Dancing Day

T0071055

A cycle of traditional Christmas Carols

Arranged for S.S.A. voices
and Harp (or Piano)

by John Rutter

Commissioned by the West Midlands Arts Association
and given its first performance in Coventry Cathedral
on 26 January 1974

MUSIC DEPARTMENT

OXFORD
UNIVERSITY PRESS

Contents

Part I	Page
Prelude	1
Angelus ad virginem	7
A virgin most pure	11
Personent Hodie	25
Part II	
Interlude	29
There is no rose	31
Coventry carol	33
Tomorrow shall be my dancing day	38

Duration 22 minutes

A separate harp part is on sale.

The vocal score is also available on hire.

for Muriel Liddle

DANCING DAY

JOHN RUTTER

Part I

PRELUDE

© Oxford University Press 1974

Printed in Great Britain
OXFORD UNIVERSITY PRESS, MUSIC DEPARTMENT, GREAT CLARENDON STREET, OXFORD OX2 6DP

Photocopying this copyright material is ILLEGAL.

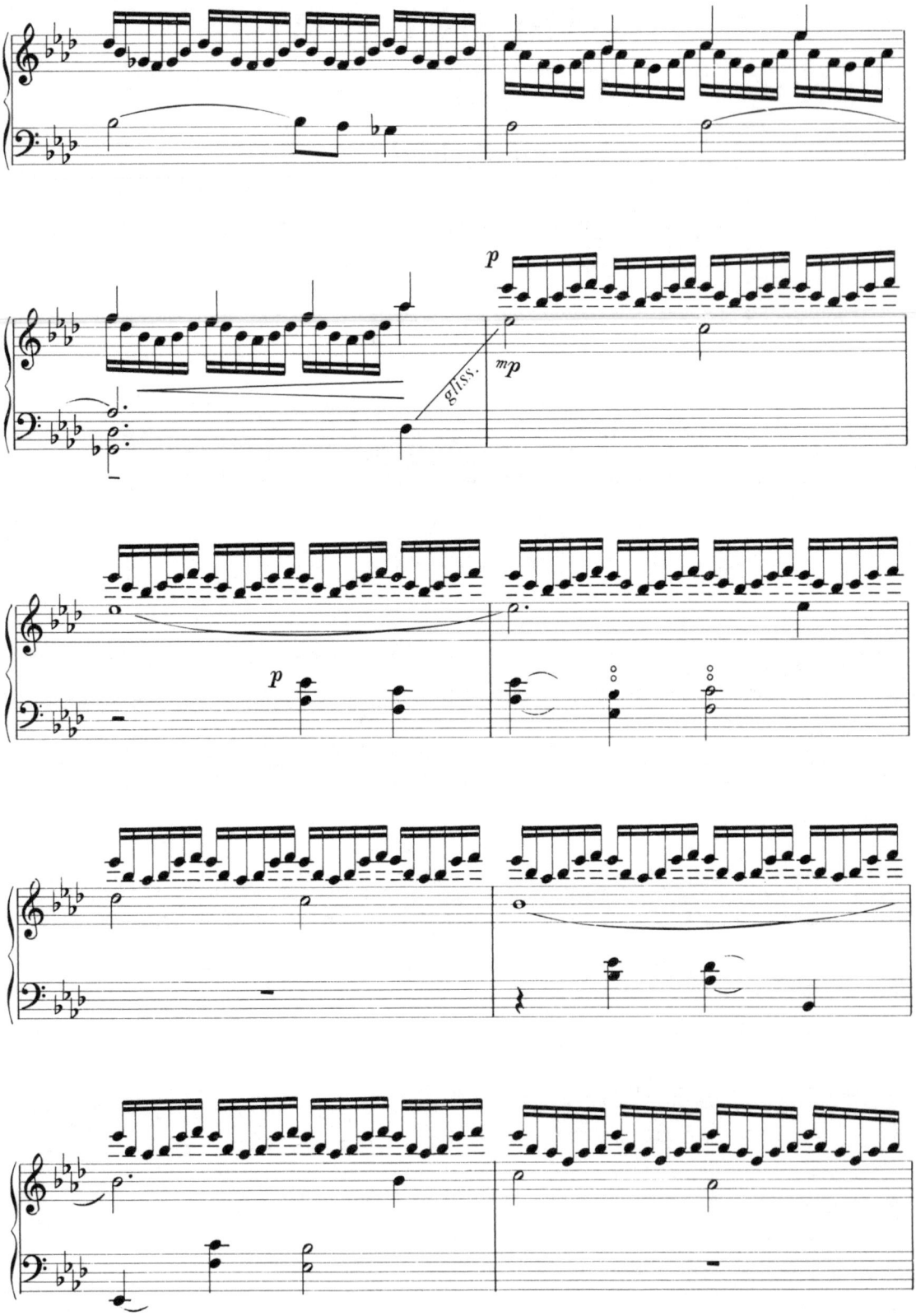
p
gliss.
mp
p

Poco più mosso (♩ = c. 108)
(mp)
G♮
G♭
G♮
8va
3
3
mf cantabile

G♭
G♮
8va
dim.
pp
8va
G♭
accelerando
8va
cresc. poco a poco
♩= c. 126
8va
(mf)
Meno mosso
(♩= c. 92)
p cresc.
f
C♯
accelerando
brillante

(♩= 126)
Largamente (♩= 96)
gliss.
ff
sonore
F♯
C♮ F♮
8va
D♮
brillante
D♭
allarg. molto
cresc.
fff
più mosso (♩=c. 112)
cresc. poco a poco
sub. p
f

accelerando
cresc.
C♭ F♭
8va
(♩ = c. 120)
ff
mp cresc.
C♮ F♮
Tempo I (♩ = c. 96)
f dim. poco a poco
p dim.
(♩. = ♩ of previous)
(attacca)
pp
cresc.
G♮

1. ANGELUS AD VIRGINEM

Words and melody
14th century

VERSE 2
mf più legato
S. 1
2. Th'an - gel to the Vir - gin said, En - t'ring in - to her bo - wer, For
mf più legato
S. 2
2. Th'an - gel to the Vir - gin said, En - t'ring in - to her bo - wer, For
mf più legato
A.
2. Th'an- gel to the Vir - gin said, En - t'ring in - to her bo - wer, For
mf
Tacet or play colla voce
dread of qua-king of this maid, He said 'Hail', with great ho - nou - re. 'Hail!' be thou
dread of qua-king of this maid, He said 'Hail', with great ho - nou - re. 'Hail!' be thou
dread of qua-king of this maid, He said 'Hail', with great ho- nou - re. 'Hail!' be thou

B
queen of mai-dens mo, Lord of hea - ven and earth al - so, Con -
queen of mai - dens mo, Lord of hea - ven and earth al - so, Con -
queen of mai - dens mo, Lord of hea - ven and earth al - so, Con -
G♭
G♮
- ceive thou shalt, And bear with-al the Lord of might, heal of all man-
- ceive thou shalt, And bear with-al the Lord of might, heal of all man -
- ceive thou shalt, And bear with-al the Lord of might, heal of all man-
G♭
G♮

-kind. He will make the gate_of hea-ven bright, Med-'cine of all our_ sin.'
-kind. He will make the gate_of hea-ven bright, Med-'cine of all our_ sin.'
-kind. He will make the gate_of hea-ven bright, Med-'cine of all our_ sin.'
G♭
G♮

VERSE 3

mf SOPRANOS
3. 'Quo-mo-do con-ci-pe-rem Quae vi-rum non co-gno-vi? Qua-li-ter in-
mf
SOPRANOS
f and ALTOS
-frin-ge-rem Quod fir-ma-men-te vo-vi?' 'Spi-ri-tus
f
G♭

2. A VIRGIN MOST PURE

Words and melody
English traditional

cresc.
pro - phets do tell, Hath brought forth a_ ba - by, as it hath be - fel, To
cresc.
3
mf
mp
be our Re - deem-er from death, hell, and sin, Which_ A - dam's_ trans-
mf
mp
A♮
A♭
A
SOPRANOS
f and ALTOS
-gres - sion hath wrap - pèd us in: Aye and there-fore_ be_ mer - ry, re -
f
mf
- joice and be you mer - ry, Set sor - rows_ a - side; Christ Je - sus_ our_
mf
A♮
A♭

VERSE 2
SOPRANOS and ALTOS
mf
Sa-viour was born on this tide.
2. At Beth-lem in
Db
Jew-ry a ci-ty there was, Where Jo-seph and Ma-ry to-ge-ther did
Dh
Db
Dh
3
pass, And there to be tax-èd with ma-ny one mo', For
Ah
Ab
B
f Unis.
Cae-sar com-man-ded the same should be so: Aye and there-fore be
f

mer - ry, re - joice and be you mer - ry, Set sor - rows_ a - side; Christ_
A♮
A♭

Je - sus_ our_ Sa - viour was born on this tide.
mp
D♭
D♮
D♭
D♮

VERSE 3

S. 1
mp
3. But _ when they had en - tered the ci - ty so fair, _ A
S. 2
mp
3. But _ when_ they_ had en - tered the ci - ty so fair, A _
A.
mp
3. But when they had en - tered the ci - ty so fair, A _
Tacet or play colla voce
D♭
D♮

num-ber of peo-ple so migh-ty was there, That Jo-seph and Ma-ry, whose
num-ber of peo-ple so migh-ty was there, That Jo-seph and Ma-ry, whose
num-ber of peo-ple so migh-ty was there, That Jo-seph and Ma-ry, whose
D♭
D♮

©
sub-stance was small, Could find in the inn there no lod-ging at
sub-stance was small, Could find in the inn there no lod-ging at
sub-stance was small, Could find in the inn there no lod-ging at
A♮
A♭
D♭
D♮

©
mf
all: Aye and there-fore be mer-ry, re-joice and be you mer-ry, Set
all: Aye and there-fore be mer-ry, re-joice and be you mer-ry, Set
all: Aye and there-fore be mer-ry, re-joice and be you mer-ry, Set
sor-rows a-side; Christ Je-sus our Sa-viour was born on this tide.
sor-rows a-side; Christ Je-sus our Sa-viour was born on this tide.
sor-rows a-side; Christ Je-sus our Sa-viour was born on this tide.
mp
A♮
A♭
D♭
D♮
D♭

VERSE 4

SOPRANO or ALTO SOLO

* A cut may be made from here to the asterisk at the bottom of p. 20.

VERSE 5
p dolce
S. 1 2
SOLO or TUTTI
mp dolce
Ah
Ah
A.
5. The King of all glo-ry to the world be-ing brought, Small store of fine
r.h. tacet ad lib.
p
D♭
D♮
Ah
3
Ah
li-nen to wrap him was sought; And when she had swad-dled her young son so
A♮
E
(p)
Ah
Ah
TUTTI
mp
sweet, With-in an ox-man-ger she laid him to sleep: Aye and
p
A♭
D♭
D♮

Ah
there - fore be_ mer - ry, re - joice and be you mer - ry, Set sor - rows_ a -
A♮
Ah
- side; Christ Je - sus_ our_ Sa - viour was born on this tide.
mp
A♭
D♭
* VERSE 6
mp
S.1
SOLO or TUTTI
Ah
mf
S.2
6. Then God sent_ an_ an - gel from hea - ven so high, To_ cer - tain_ poor_
A.
mp
Ah
Ah
*
Tacet (for rehearsal only)
D♮
D♭

Ah
Ah
shep-herds in fields where they lie, And bade them no long-er in
Ah
D♮

F
Ah
sor - row to stay, Be - cause that our Sa- viour was born on this
Ah
A♮
A♭
D♭
D♮

F
f
Aye and there-fore be mer-ry, re-joice and be you mer-ry, Set
day. Aye and there-fore be mer-ry, re-joice and be you mer-ry, Set
Aye and there-fore be mer-ry, re-joice and be you mer-ry, Set
(8va higher ad lib.)
sor-rows a-side; Christ Je-sus our Sa-viour was born on this tide.
sor-rows a-side; Christ Je-sus our Sa-viour was born on this tide.
sor-rows a-side; Christ Je-sus our Sa-viour was born on this tide.
A♮
A♭
D♭
D♮
D♭

VERSE 7
S. 1
S. 2 nd A.
f
7. Then pre - sent-ly the shep-herds did
7. Then pre - sent- ly af - ter, the shep - herds did
sonore
spy A num - ber of an - gels in the sky;
spy A num - ber of an - gels that stood in the sky; They
They talk - èd, and sweet - ly did sing,
joy - ful- ly talk - èd, and sweet - ly did sing, To

G
ff
To God be all glo - ry. Aye and there-fore be
God be all glo - ry, our hea - ven-ly King. Aye and there-fore be
D♮
mer - ry; re - joice and be you mer - ry, Set sor - rows a -
mer - ry, re - joice and be you mer - ry, Set sor - rows a -
sim.
A♮
allargando
- side; Christ Je - sus our Sa - viour was born on this tide.
- side; Christ Je - sus our Sa - viour was born on this tide.
A♭
D♭

3. PERSONENT HODIE

Words and melody from
Piae Cantiones (1582)

SOPRANOS
mf
2. In mun-do na-sci-tur, Pan-nis in - vol-vi-tur, Prae-se-pi po-ni-tur
Verse 2
Sta-bu-lo bru-to-rum, Rec-tor su-per-no-rum. Per-di-dit -dit, -dit,
D♭
B
Per-di-dit, -dit, -dit, Per-di-dit spo-li-a prin-ceps in-fer-no-rum.
D♮
S. 1 2
mp
3. Ma-gi tres ve-ne-runt, Par-vu-lum
A.
mp
3. Ma-gi tres ve-ne-runt, Par-vu-lum
Verse 3
mp
Tacet - for rehearsal only

S.1
in-qui-runt, Beth-le-hem ad-e-unt, Stel-lu-lam se-quen-do,
S.2
in-qui-runt, Beth-le-hem ad-e-unt, Stel-lu-lam se-
A.
in-qui-runt, Beth-le-hem ad-e-unt, Stel-lu-lam se-
Ip-sum a-do-ran-do, Au-rum, thus, thus, thus, Au-rum, thus,
-quen-do, Ip-sum a-do-ran-do, Au-rum, thus, thus, thus, Au-rum,
-quen-do, Ip-sum a-do-ran-do, Au-rum, thus, thus, thus, Au-rum,
thus, thus, Au-rum, thus, et myrr-ham e-i of-fe-ren-do.
thus, thus, Au-rum, thus, et myrr-ham e-i of-fe-ren-do.
thus, thus, Au-rum, thus, et myrr-ham e-i of-fe-ren-do.
p

SOPRANOS and ALTOS
f
4. Om-nes cle - ri-cu-li, Pa-ri-ter
mf cresc.
f
(A♮)
A♭
E♮
unis.
pu-e ri, Can-tent ut an-ge-li: Ad-ve-ni-sti mun-do,
E♭
A♮
D
cresc.
ff
Lau-des ti-bi fun-do. I-de-o, -o, -o, I-de-o,
cresc.
ff
A♭
allargando
-o, -o, I-de-o glo-ri-a in ex-cel-sis De-o.
8va
gliss.
F major
A♮
E♮

Part II

INTERLUDE

mp
p
liberamente
e declamato
8va
f
marcato
(8va)
ff
laissez vibrer
(8va)
dim.
p
pp
Tempo giusto
molto tranquillo
dolce e
legato
p
pp
p

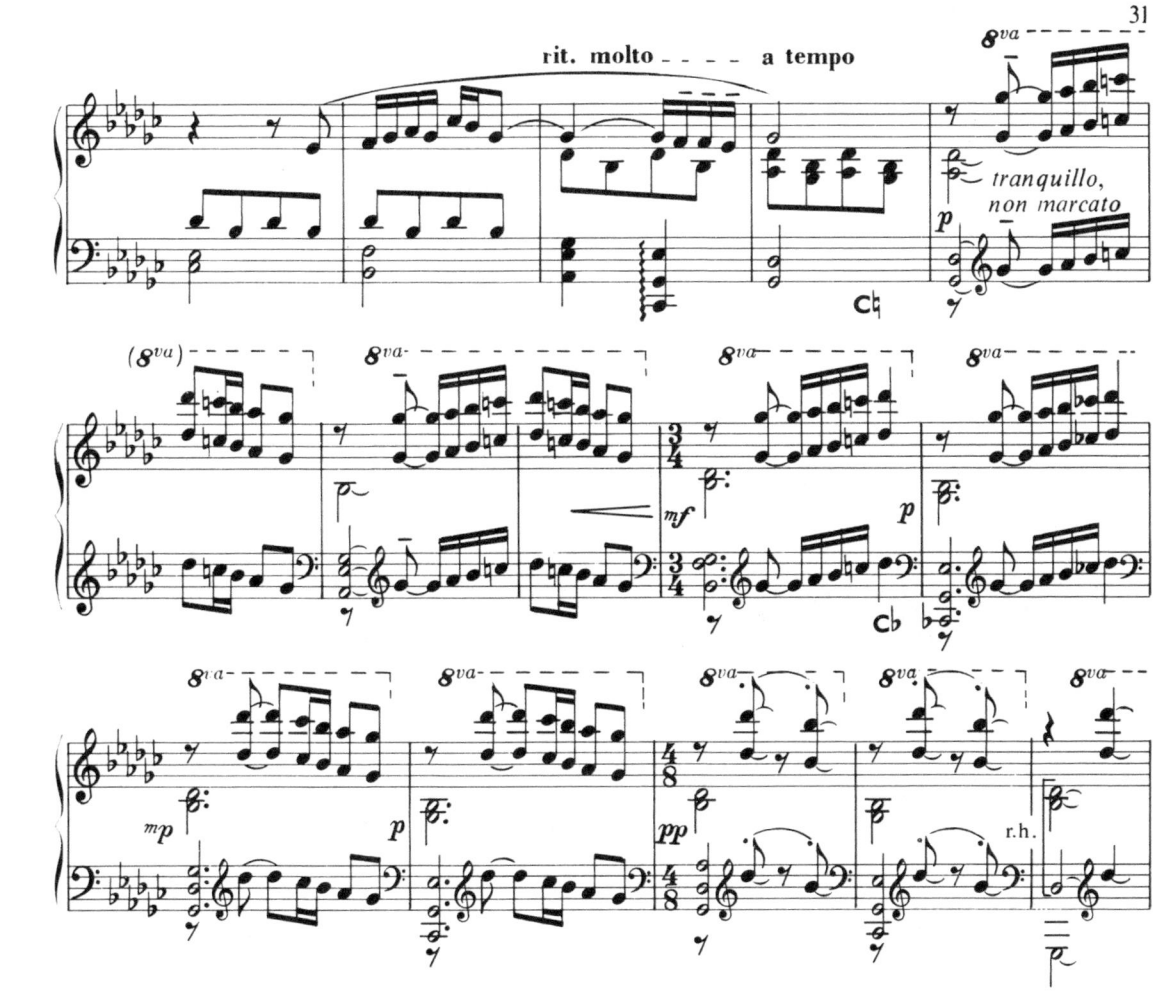

4. THERE IS NO ROSE

Voice parts and words
15th century *

* From the edition by John Stevens by permission of Stainer & Bell Ltd.

As is the rose that bare Je - su.
mp
p
VERSES 1 and 2
mf dolce
S.
Soli 1. There is no rose of such vir - tue As
All 2. For in this rose con - tain - èd was Hea -
mf dolce
A.
is the rose that bare Je - su. Al - le -
-ven and earth in lit - tle space. Res mi -
D. S. for Verse 2
- lu - - - - - ia.
- ran - - - - - da.

5. COVENTRY CAROL

Words from the Pageant of the Shearmen and Tailors, 15th century

Voice parts slightly adapted from a Ms. of 1591

Andante con moto (♩ = c. 96)

p mesto e legato
Lul - ly, lul - la, thou lit - tle ti-ny child, By by, lul - ly, lul -
p mesto e legato
p
D♭, A♮
A♭
A♮
A♭
D♮
- lay, thou lit - tle ti-ny child, By by, lul - ly, lul - lay.
C♯
C♮ D♭
A♮
D♮
VERSE 1
mp
1. O sis- ters too, How may we do For to pre - serve this day This
mp
mp
D♭
A♭
A♮
A♭
D♮
C♯

For whom we do sing,
poor young-ling For whom we do sing, By by, lul - ly lul - lay?
For whom we do sing,
C♮, D♭
A♮
D♮
A♭
VERSE 2
f marcato
S.
A.
2. He - rod the king, In his ra - ging, Char - ged he
simile
f
mf
D♭, G♮
hath this day His men of might, In his own
f
f
sim.
E♮, A♮

mf cresc.
ff
sight, All young chil - dren to slay.
mp cresc.
ff
D♮, E♭
VERSE 3
p legato
3. That woe is me, Poor child for_ thee! And ev - er
p legato
p cantabile e legato
D♭, G♭
A♭
A♮ G♮
A♭ G♭
mp
morn and_ day, For thy part - ing Nei-ther say nor_
mp
mp
D♭
D♮

A
p
pp
sing By by, lul - ly lul - lay! Lul - ly, lul -
A♮
D♮
- la, thou lit - tle ti-ny child, By by, lul - ly, lul -
A♭ D♭
A♮
A♭
D♮
mp
pp
- lay, thou lit - tle ti-ny child, By by, lul - ly, lul - lay.
D♭
A♮
D♮
A♭

6. TOMORROW SHALL BE MY DANCING DAY

Words and melody
English traditional

SOLO SOPRANO
(or SEMI-CHORUS)
mf
1. To - mor - row shall be my danc - ing day: I would my
p
true love did so chance To see the le - gend of my play, To
3
f
call my true love to my dance: Sing O my love, O my
mf
dim.
mp
mf
love, my love, my love; This have I done for my true love. To -
A
ALL VOICES
f
dim.
p
mp

- mor- row shall be my danc - ing day: I would my true love did so
f
chance To see the le - gend of my play, To call my true love
mf
3
mf
to my dance: Sing O my love, O my love, my
f
f
dim.
dim.
love, my love; This have I done for my true love.
mp
mf
cresc.
f
L.H.
mp
mf
mp leggiero

VERSE 2
S.1
mf legato
2. Then was I born of a vir - gin
S.2
mf legato
2. Then was I born of a
S.1
pure, Of her I took flesh - ly sub - stance; Thus was I
S.2
vir-gin pure, I took flesh - ly sub - stance; Thus was I
A.
mf legato
2. Of her I took flesh - ly sub - stance; Thus was I
B
knit to man's na - ture, To call my true love to my
knit to man's na - ture, To call my true love to my
knit to man's na - ture, To call my true love to my

B
f
dim.
dance: Sing O my_ love, O___ my love, my love, my
f
dim.
dance: Sing O my_ love, my love, sing___ O___
f
dim.
dance: Sing___ O my love, sing_ O___my love,___ sing___ O___
mf
mp
love; This have I done_for my___ true love.
mp
___ my love; This have I done for my true love.
mp
___ my love;___ This have I done for my true love.
mp
mf

VERSE 3
S. 1
S. 2
A.
mf
Ah
3. In a man - ger laid and wrapp'd I
was, So ve - ry poor, this was my chance, Be - twixt an
Ah
Ah
Ah
Sing
ox and a sil - ly poor ass, To call my true love to my dance:
Sing
(mf)
3

©
dim.
p
cresc.
O my_ love, O___ my love, my love, my love, This
O my love, O my love,_ my love,_ my love, This
O my love, O my love, my love, my love, This
dim.
p
mf
have I done_ for my_ true love.
have I done for my true love.
have I done_ for my true love.
cresc.
mf
f
Gb
C# F#

D
ALL VOICES
f
To - mor - row shall be my
8va
cresc.
ff
ritmico
f
C♮ F♮ G♮
danc - ing day: I would my true love did so chance To
see the le - gend of my play, To call my true love
E
ff
dim.
S. 1
to my dance: Sing O my love, O my
S. 2
A.
ff
dim.
to my dance: Sing O my love, O my love, my
ff
dim.

Reproduced and printed by
Halstan & Co. Ltd., Amersham, Bucks., England